EYE LEVEL

The University of Massachusetts Press   Amherst 1977

Jane Shore EYE LEVEL

For my parents

Either the Darkness alters—
Or something in the sight
Adjusts itself to Midnight—
And Life steps almost straight.
—Emily Dickinson
  419

I would like to express my gratitude to the Radcliffe Institute for its support during the inception of this book, and to the Massachusetts Endowment for the Arts and Humanities, which supported its completion.

Versions of many of these poems first appeared in the following periodicals and anthologies: *Poetry*: This World without Miracles, Ararat, The Glass Paperweight, Animals That Die in Our Houses, An Astronomer's Journal, Landing Off Season, The Princess and the Pea, The Sniper as Axis Mundi, Landscape with Trees, The Sleeper Watched: Three Studies, The Anniversary, and A Letter Sent to Summer. *The American Review*: Dieting. *The Iowa Review*: Noon and Doors. *The Antioch Review*: Epigram of the Smothering Lover. *Audience*: Home Movies: 1949, The Lifeguard, The Necklace of Anger, and Mud Season: Vermont. *Ploughshares*: Constantly. *The New Republic*: Fortunes Pantoum and Witness. *padan aram*: Skating. *The Ohio Journal*: Survival Tactics. *The Harvard Advocate*: Iowa Spring Viewed from a Plane. *Best Poems of 1973: The Borestone Mountain Poetry Awards*: Ararat. *Best Poems of 1975: The Borestone Mountain Poetry Awards*: Animals That Die in Our Houses. *The Blacksmith Anthology*: Sounding the Lake. *Ten American Poets: An Anthology of Poems*: The Lifeguard, Ararat, Landing Off Season, and Mud Season: Vermont. *Out of this World: Poems from the Hawkeye State*: Iowa Spring Viewed from a Plane.

Special thanks to Barry and Lorrie Goldensohn, Roger Weingarten, Norman Dubie, Mekeel McBride, Bob Grenier, and to Dean Cummins who showed me the eyeless fish.

Contents

ONE

Witness

Chilled moonrise, his mother now in bed,
her terror tranquilizing with the cold idea—
we scoured the neighborhood with searchlights,
the woods behind his school; the lumberyard's
cesspool, a black moon in the grass, called
everyone and no one, called to me.
Jackknifed in the pipe, he could not shimmy up
the mud and ooze, the narrow walls collapsing,
dark water notching up his spine.
Did he see me swimming in the glazed eye
of light he woke to, did he wake at all,
as the icy noose of water tightened around
his chin? The north star of the squad car
flashing. Navigating by touch and shadow,
our lasso caught his feet. We tugged.
His head slipped deeper in the cavity.
Helpless, I held my breath. Hand over hand,
we hauled him up and out into the humming air:
limp and shivering, feet-first.
He swung a long moment over us, shiny,
bigger than we thought, his face bruised blue
by that metallic light. Cold gravity; release.
He whined like nothing human in my arms.

The Advent Calendar

For Peggy Rizza

1:

Outside the bay windows
the sky fills up with snow.
The pentangular wall of night
reflects my reading lamp
into a constellation.
My neighbor glancing in
can see just one lamp shining.

The calendar windows
seal off a winter landscape too.
Skaters glide across a pond
over the round window in the ice.
Behind the shutters of a stall
an aproned carpenter
sweeps sawdust into a pile
barely enough to fill a thimble.

A child peers through
the bakery window.
I slit along the window frame,
lifting the boy
and the glass wall of tortes
off into a prophecy . . .
As the window swings open
the boy begins to see himself
up to his elbows in flour
beside the pyramid of loaves.
Is the night wind sifting the flour?
Has the blizzard turned the kitchen
inside out?
—Like a cloud passing through
the baker's heart,
his beard goes snowy white.

Oh woman in the foreground
with your beautiful skirts,
do you contain a window too—
like the church's arched door
opening on a nave of tiny worshippers?
Behind the clerestory window

a creche appears—
the madonna mobbed by putti,
the infant
cushioned on the backs of sheep.

Madonna of the Beautiful Skirts,
you carried into Egypt
within your body
a world of such belief!
I can only carry
myself into my life.
In my windowed room, only I
am multiplied
and pray to be whole.

These lives I randomly
release into the world
like doves!

In seconds I do it!
My light unlocks the stalls,
two dozen and one windows open—
all, except the window of the moon,
already painted on as shining.

I used to wish those 25 days
would vanish, a miracle!
But would hurrying
break the spell,
would the windows turn real
and shatter in my eyes?

Better to shut them,
keep the future out,
as this last window
of the moon stays shut.
But who can resist
the moon's bright eye
in this paper sky,
or any other?

Once, looking for the moon,
at the far end
of the telescope, I saw
the echo of my own dark eye
shining. The more I tried
to take the glass away, the more
that eye deepened into mine,
burning beyond the human shape
the self takes on.

Can light be so intense
the future's in a glance?
If I hold my hand to light,
the bright lattice of my bones
shines through.

3:              In the night sky, stars are falling.
I open the crescent window of the moon.
Inside, a man is hiking in sheer daylight
clear across Tibet where it is day.
The mountain peaks break in yellow waves
and the man is walking unconcerned
on a tide of birds.
Morning lies behind this window,
the window of sunrise;
its movement over the world
arrives always with gifts in both arms.

The Glass
Paperweight

1:

Over the rooftops the city's green horizon
shines through the terrarium on the sill.
My plants flourish in their tropics.
The green smell of weather
is the way life smells, an oasis breathing.

Who navigated the ship into the bottle
or the message in the bottle
that reads *rescue* and *island*?
Before my windows I lean out like a figurehead,
against the glass as against a great wind.
In the mind of the island's one survivor
the rescuer is always sailing, toward
his other self, who swims to meet him.

Is the paperweight,
this blizzard in my palm,
my own dream of escape?
Inside, a man splits logs
the width of toothpicks.
Snow falls through the liquid air.
Or the snow has just fallen
and the sky is clear.

A carved backdrop of 'Swiss Alps'
bleeds a blue stripe
down the careful line of evergreens
and continues melting onto the cottage roof.
Beneath, I imagine, something good is cooking.
Decaled on the kitchen window,
a woman's face.
Smoke hangs over her tiny chimney
like a parachute that never lands.
Throughout the snowstorm
there is a sunset going on
as the woman watches the child in the sled
whose cap is coated
with the identical blue alp.

A snowstorm is always about to happen.
Here is a country under siege.
The children in the cottage
feel the world tip over,
and with an astronaut's notion of gravity,
turn over in their beds and dream.
But the child in the sled in the paperweight
is always caught outside
regardless of the weather.

He stares at the sky
that is always collapsing
and sees my magnified lunar face rise,
wishing the light or my hand's heatwave
would melt the immutable snow.

I stare through the glass an inch away

pressed against the window
like the mother calling to her child.

If only she could unglue her mouth
from the glass
where her breath sticks
like frost on the pane,
if only the sound could leave her mouth
the way a locomotive
shoots from a mountain tunnel,
then the order of their silence
would break with my cry
moving its bat-perfect sonar
through the climate of their sorrow.
Frozen in that lit interior,
who will warn them
when the bad weather will begin?
Who will bring the child in?

**Animals That Die
in Our Houses**

A cat once walked off the roof into our garden
landing like a table on all fours.
We found a field mouse curled on linoleum
with paws drawn up
in an attitude of prayer.

In the clear balloon of the fishbowl
the goldfish makes perfect breathy O's.
One fish, in that watery stratosphere
where the water is thin and dangerous,
floats upside-down like a flag in distress.

Locked in that lunatic position,
the fish is a moon out of orbit,
out of grace with gravity; World,
it has turned its back on you completely
and is wed to its new element, the sky.

What laws govern our houses,
our civilized many-roomed coffins above ground,
that invite these creatures to tunnel or chew
into our lives? Are ears and noses caves,
environments the insects find hospitable,

as in helicoptic circles they navigate
our sleeping heads? Is it accidental,
then, how they seem to swim closer to us in death,
or fall out of the sky like small
oddly shaped chunks of heaven.

They occupy our lives so briefly,
the insect rocking in the bowl of its shell,
the fish pumped up to the water's breakable surface,
in death appear more innocent
than the shapes our minds invent.

Imposing on us a kind of isolation,
they seem much more human than we are;
when solitary and cautious, they watch us
lie in our formal positions
in the deep grass, in the woods, together.

**A Letter Sent
to Summer**

Oh summer if you would only come
with your big baskets of flowers,
dropping by like an old friend
just passing through the neighborhood!

If you came to my door disguised
as a thirsty biblical angel
I'd buy all your hairbrushes and magazines!
I'd be more hospitable
than any ancient king.

I'd personally carry your luggage in.
Your monsoons. Your squadrons of bugs.
Your plums and lovely melons.
Let the rose let out its long long sigh.
And Desire return to the hapless rabbit.

This request is also in my own behalf.
Inside my head it is always snowing,
even when I sleep. When I wake up,
and still you have not arrived,
I curl back into my blizzard of linens.

Not like winter's buckets of whitewash.
Please wallpaper my bedroom
with leafy vegetables and farms.
If you knocked right now,
I would not interfere.
Start near the window.
Start right here.

Skating

Red flag up—
    the lake is frozen over,
    safe for the children now
who wear ski masks, monster faces, or faces
you might encounter in outer space:
    woolly skulls—sleek, hooded;
    cut-out ovals and diamonds
edged in red rickrack are portholes for the senses.

Puffing out
    hot mouthfuls of air,
    they are chugging
like locomotives on the track to the lake.
Once I was one of them:
    stuffed, zipped into my parka,
    so insulated against the cold
I couldn't feel a thing lacing up my skates.

Teetering,
    my sawtooth blade-tips catch
    on the slatted wooden ramps,
and the world goes horizontal, the world
is this flat sheet of ice.
    Wind at my back
    like a large impersonal hand
sends me skidding off to where the island is.

The whole island
    is no bigger than a living room.
    Beneath me, cracks appear
where the ice is smoothest, blackest, thinnest—
a palm print, a screen of melting radar.
    Oh, the lake is calling
    to its banks. It sounds
like a birdcall, but in a deeper, more human voice.

But this is
    the lake's response to the skaters
    who think the lake is glass.
It does look like a piece of Steuben glass!

Milky bubbles of air, like large eggs,
    are frozen in it.
    Once, a boy fell in,
was fished out, fly in an ice cube, his scarf

wrapped frozen
    around his neck. This is
    the way I remember
the story, though I never saw the boy.
When I search for the spot he drowned in,
    when I try to find
    his face, I see
my own face, a small Atlantis rising to the surface,

trying to break
    through. Not a child's face
    but the face of a woman
who has been a stranger for thirty years.
I skate in my sleep and I look,
    at my own risk,
    the red flag down—
all memory under.

Constantly

I woke, for an instant,
not knowing you.
Before touch, before

the thought of touch.
In the level darkness
I could locate

nothing of you,
no manacle of outline,
and I thought

how, each morning, the body
wakes to recognize
its shape, again

the tender landscape
given, the strangeness
of the right hand

orbiting the side,
the wrists where pulse
can quicken at a word.

And the body,
fluent in its element,
is water that the dailiness

of life runs over.
Now this, now
that: heartbeat,

the pupil widening
to light, admits
what's attended to—

a chair mimics
the woman seated,
cup's handle accepts

her hand. The body
receptive also, and birds
occupy the ear.

In darkness, the eye
shapes its constellation.
The hand

traces. Two fish
swim in their starry
perimeters; but the bird's

song's instinct,
a template in the brain.
Never let me fix you

ever, be the cloud
constantly inventing
its body like a dream

passing through your eye,
each morning dreaming
the sky a moment earlier

to light, skimming the sudden
unfamiliar coast.
And below the coast,

in the clearest water
senses can distill, here,
before love, touch returns

us to that density
silence roots the very
center of.

TWO

Ararat

Somebody said the sea would come to us
cutting like an army through wheat—
its captive women, dolphins in the wake
of our little boat. As water drains
every wife's a sea-wife. Such traffic
you would think it market day!
Hooked to their elbows, baskets
of apricots and limes,
anchor the widows in the muddy slopes
where the world begins. The elements
have never been more married.

I have grown to love tending this garden
that barks and coos in the moonlight
when there is a moon.
Spindly giraffes cluster at the bow.
Ants inch down the plank in twos.
The sheep are nervous. Their thick wool
steams as the dew burns off.

Crises crush men more. In sleep
my husband's pitchy hands hammer the air
as if another boat could float us back
to who we were. I imagine
I am the mountain he teeters on
as every wave of wind comes past.
I watch for clouds.

Second Story Sunlight

1:

Our driveway
joined the butchershop
and the bakery.
Two stories up, dressing
for school, I saw
the slaughterhouse truck
deliver sides of beef,
rib cages, stiff carcasses
it took two men to lift.
A shield of blood—
the butcher's apron.
Surgical white cases;
glistening ovals
of liver on waxed paper.

The butcher fed the meat grinder
a dark pound of chuck.
On the sharpening steel,
he tuned his instruments:
the cleaver's one low note,
his row of carving knives
ran up the scale.

Behind the counter
stretched along the wall,
a half-dozen rabbits hung.
Skinned and earless,
their long bodies
were shiny as a yard
of shantung.
They looked like the picture
in the biology book—
the baby was slippery,
still attached
by the twisted cord.

A corridor of arctic air
blew in the room.
The smell of blood
on the butcher's hands.

I tried to focus
on the scale window
and saw the meat
transform to numbers
bounced and spun.

2:        Turned out of Eden,
I was Adam
naming the animals.
I was Eve naming my sons.
Pain had been invented,
the first division of labor.
The sons I raised
raised sheep and grain.
And time was measured
by the workshift
on either side of me
dividing night from day.

3:
In the deep night
the bakery lights lit red
my bedroom's blue west wall.

The exhaust fan hummed.
The gigantic hunger
of the dough machine's
empty drum revolving.

Shouts punctuate the air.
Something slapped,
punched into shape
with all the violence
of flesh being mollified.

I knew by heart
what came next.
In the limits of space
and air, a silence
locked in the imprint
of the baker's hands.

4:     I imagined the cake decorator
       at his bench, his cap
       a punctured cloud.
       His pastry bag
       squeezed out
       small baroque perfections
       again and again.
       A cornice. The upper
       stories of the cake.
       On the roof he looped
       his penmanship
       and placed
       the child's saints,
       those soldiers of matrimony,
       in ionic porticos.

       When suddenly I smelled
       bread rising, coming
       from the walls!
       Pumpernickel, Vienna, Rye.
       They smelled so good
       I couldn't separate
       the sweet dough from the sour,
       this converging, neutral
       humanity of smell,
       not animal, not vegetable.
       Flesh that is not flesh,
       that can be eaten . . .

5:         On the other side of the world,
          young girls prepare for bed
          or come home from school,

          as I rise,
          they bend under the sun.
          Ankle-deep in rice paddies,
          carrying brothers and sisters
          on their backs,

          squatting to pound grain
          into a mortar,
          your bodies grow
          the way a level field of wheat
          rises from the landscape
          in unison;

          with just this common
          bread between us
          men toil over
          and break,
          bread the world has risen from,
          the labor we prepare for
          even now.

Home Movies:
1949

Woozy from death they hog the camera
that revives them, blinking like children
we shook awake. Intensities of plaid
coagulate on screen. One distant cousin.
Above the picnic baskets, bobbing
like icebergs they investigate the silence
each time we run them through the same
embarrassing routines. I am swimming.
In the river father's trousers cling,
two drooping cylinders. He stumbles
toward us, digs deep, retrieves a cowbone.
Thrusts it like a barbell above his head.
Soloing, my uncle handles his trombone
careful as dentures. Next to me his widow
stiffens. An aunt glides by with a thermos.
We are kept always out of earshot,
safe. Clutching their trophies they wave
us off. I forget how cold the water was.

Noon

For Susan

Along the creek girls are lifting
their thin skirts and as they bend
low, under their loose scoop-neck
blouses the pale flesh shows.
They notice you and wave, turn back
again laughing, dipping their feet
into the cool water. Now scarves go;
they unpin their hair. On the banks
the grass turns down like sheets
and the sun is big and close.
You can barely see them through
the heat as they peel and peel away
their clothes. And when they open
their slender arms to you thinking
they are doing this because they
want to, thinking there is a choice,
who can blame them for giving in
this easily, or you, nearer now
to yourself than ever as they pull
you with them, sister, down.

The Princess
and the Pea

Asway on top of my tower of mattresses,
my Tibet, the stars are allies as they die
perfect and sudden in the corner of my eye.
Speech floats up to me in streamers. My hair
fans out. Below, the village children sleep
insular as bears. Daybreak when I descend
these soft cliffs, all will amaze
at my bruised authentic skin, the acceptance
of pain with grace. I question only this:
that the stubborn knot I lie on
is genuine as a cultured pearl,
gritty against the teeth, but not a pearl.
I lie in my skin as in an ugly coat:
my body owned by the citizens
who ache and turn whenever I turn
on the pea on which so much depends.

Lot's Wife

God evicts his tenants
on such short notice
who knew
what to take?
My husband, my daughters
loaded down
with things, things, only I
lagged behind.

Old men used to come to me
to pray and weep
and pull their long white beards
and the fringe
on their prayer shawls
as if I were the Wailing Wall.

If only I were the Wailing Wall
with a tenement of weeds
in my wrinkles.

Salt.
Magic in the lunchrooms
of public schools! Tricks!
A child balancing
a salt shaker
on one salt crystal.
I'm now that small.
Smaller than that.

I saw the dark rushing overhead
and the brimstone
flipping through the air
like fistfuls of coins.
They bounced on the ground.
They rolled on their edges.

If I said *manna*
it would be a lie.
All that shining!

I only wanted
to stuff my dress
with souvenirs. Evidence
I'd been there.

An Astronomer's Journal

Even in sleep my eyes are on the elements.
My eyes are pencils being perpetually resharpened
puzzling out the sky's connecting dots
one almost expects to be accompanied by numbers,
jig-saw animal-shaped constellations,
bear, bent dipper, wed fish in repose,
crowding out the angels who I suppose
must be stacked up tier on tier
as in the horseshoe of the opera house.
Each night the sky splits open like a melon
its starry filaments
the astronomer examines with great intensity.
Caught in his expensive glass eye
more microscope than telescope,
it is his own eye he sees, reflected
and possessed, a moon-disc in a lake,
safe, even to himself, untouchable;
and so his notion of himself must be corrected:
"Actually, the universe is introspective."

Fortunes Pantoum

You will go on a long journey
You will have a happy and healthy life
You will recover valuables thought lost
You will marry and have many children

You will have a happy and healthy life
Your sweetheart will always be faithful
You will marry and have many children
You will have many friends when you need them

Your sweetheart will always be faithful
Soon you will come into a large inheritance
You will have many friends when you need them
You will succeed in your line of work

Soon you will come into a large inheritance
You will travel to many new places
You will succeed in your line of work
Be suspicious of well-meaning strangers

You will travel to many new places
A message from a distance is soon to be received
Be suspicious of well-meaning strangers
Important news from an unexpected source!

A message from a distance is soon to be received
You will meet a dark and handsome foreigner
Important news from an unexpected source!
Do not take unnecessary chances

You will meet a dark and handsome foreigner
You have a fear of visiting high places
Do not take unnecessary chances
Your misunderstanding will be cleared up in time

You have a fear of visiting high places
Grasp at the shadow and lose the substance
Your misunderstanding will be cleared up in time
Sometimes you worry too much about death

Grasp at the shadow and lose the substance
You will recover valuables thought lost
Sometimes you worry too much about death
You will go on a long journey

An Astronaut's Journal

Because we landed on the moon, all Americans
can walk a little taller.
Planting our carpet roll of flags,
fifty miniature silk flags,
one for each state in the Union!
I feel so proud of my own Garden State
with vegetables stitched onto the blue field
of sky instead of stars.

One of the seas is called Tranquillity.
Up here I am so lonely.
If only the sea would fill up with water
so I can go sailing, if only the sea
would stop acting like a cranium
always filling up with thoughts.
Then there could be a Sea of Stimulation
where boats go by but the captains
all are naked
and everyone is sunning on the decks.

But the best part of being here is
no gravity. There are drawers for "Food"
and a drawer for "Shaving." I am wondering
what to put in the "Rock Drawer"
till the others come back.
Even the painting that makes our module
make me feel less homesick
for its mountains and trees and fish
has a tree with drawers for the birds to live in;
and if I push a button marked "Sunset"
the sun drops like a nickel into its own little drawer
which locks automatically the drawer marked "Sleep now."

Doors

Not ornate mahogany or quarter-inch plywood,
not Ghiberti's doors, not
stenciled *LADIES* or *GENTLEMEN* doors.
Our doors reach their full height
when we are 21, have you ever noticed them?
Light as our shadows or our bathtub rings
or the nice smells our bodies have.

Think of the emergency exit. Think of
the first time you used it. Born,
you rammed headfirst into real air.
An enormous cat is chasing you.
Here comes a wall. Beams. Your mouth
full of cobwebs. It's easy to walk
through walls, any wall, that wall say,
into anybody's bathroom. Now we are in
Minneapolis. He's shaving.
She's towelling her hair. That look on his face
as the lather floats lazily to the sea.

Has the rat a door?
Astronauts hurl toward that perfect door
in the atmosphere. Ghosts' doors
shut instantly behind them
the way water fills the hole you make
when you jump into the Mediterranean.
Houdini's door, all the doors Freud
stuck his nose into, the opera's trap door,
the door you fall through at the gallows,
your bikini with the orange pineapples on it,
that's a door too. And the doors
slamming in the eyes of your girlfriend
when she sees you kissing someone else.
The conservationists will love you.
No need to hack up Redwood Forest.
Which is not to say you ignore
what a door 'means' symbolically.

These two electric eyes are yours.
This is your automatic entry into everything.

Epigram of the
Smothering Lover

Such delicate maneuvering. My clumsiness
comes off as grace, comes off as fast
as my hands can tug at your heavy sweater,
unzip you. It's dangerous.
Look what it invites. Houdini under ice,
chains and handcuffs,
and half the city of Detroit counting off
the seconds. Another stunt. The lead
trunk hoisted up from the river.
Empty. Crushed beneath you, kissing
you, our timing is precise.
Bless calculation. How air can last!

Dieting

Always I am full of numbers,
the sad arithmetic of my body.
Every morning I weigh my feelings in
like a heavyweight champion,
wishing my robe were satin
with my name stitched on back.
Oh, I am an enormous harbor.
Fear is in the breeze.

Where do the ounces of fat go? To China?
This is how the Christmas turkey feels
as the white meat is carved from him.
This is the loneliness of the last tooth
in the gum-plateau
when you are hungry
and the body comes on with all the commotion
of the Industrial Revolution.

This is how the skinny madonna feels
as she shies away from the angel
in Martini's *Annunciation.*
The room is full of terrible surprises
each time you walk in.
Sometimes the strangers have wings.
They're always wanting you to do them a favor.

I have never eaten at the celestial Maxims
and so escaped the embarrassment of not knowing
which fork to use.
Instead, I am sinking into your three hundred dollar mattress,
this fleecy hunk of white bread.
Remember when we ate our way through Italy?
My hair fanned out like spaghetti on the pillow
and the pensione smelled garlicky under the sheets.

I have always wanted to fall for a nomad
and be swept away like a tent.
Or be folded up neat as an altarpiece.
If only you could look at me that way!
From all sides! Cherubs dangling
from wire hangers in a soup bowl full of clouds.

All the suitcases spilled from their racks
when the train lurched near Nice.
Our heads hurt! You said:
Words are such spies. Let's eat a ham sandwich.

Oh, hot apple of my eye,
all through dinner I was starved for you!
I want to swallow your colors whole,
your ivories and lapus lazulis,
the way the sea does, the way the blind do.
I love the lime look your eyes have
this early in the morning.
You taste better than all the fresh fruit
cocktails in the world,
better than the bunch of radishes
that hangs in the still life over your bed,
better than the bronze Poseidon in Athens
which the museum guards would not let me taste
but if I did, he would taste salty,
collecting the sea for so many centuries.

Am I a cannibal?
Eating little, I digest myself.
Meanwhile, Dawn is breaking over Boston,
her rosy fingers curled like shrimp.
Picasso's omelet is singing on my plate.

THREE

The Lifeguard   The children vault the giant carpet roll
of waves, with sharp cries swing legs
wide over water. A garden of umbrellas
blooms down the stretch of beach. Far
offshore always I can spot that same
pale thumbprint of a face going under,
grown bigger as I approach, the one arm circling,
locking rigid around my neck. The other
as its fist hooks and jabs my head away.
Ear to the conch, ear to the pillow,
beneath a canopy of bathers each night
I hear the voice and pry the jaws apart,
choke on the tangle of sable hair that blurs
the dead girl's mouth: that anarchy
of breath dog-soft and still at my neck.
She calls from the water glass I drink from.
From my own throat when I swallow.

Night Flight

All night
our headlights held
the unreeling

highway. Only
the traffic of
moonlight, until

a passing car
brands its sliding
diagram of light

upon your face.
Steering into
the city limits,

I begin to
enter the world
you call your life.

All night
you checked,
rechecked the map,

smoothed like
a lace skirt
across your lap;

and now, shielding
your breasts,
the clear circuits

of red and blue—
all the routes
of your heart—

decipherable
at last!
I turn off

the dashboard's
dim constellation.
A plane

threads the darkness
of the evergreen.
Now, another

arcs over your
yard. Attentive
to an echo,

a woodthrush flits
under the eaves.
Distance is

the cautionary
bird, marking
its territory

by song.
Can you hear
your house divide

by their design?
The tree sliced
vertically by

flight, by song,
and all across
the lawn, shadows

of their invisible
fences fall.
As daylight breaks

upon the windshield,
tell me how
to locate you.

I'll call your
name and swivel
the rearview mirror

to the face you
hardly recognize
as yours, now

that the bird
is silent, empty
of all

that would
unbalance you
to flight.

**The Sleeper
Watched:
Three Studies**

"The gloom of
the mind,
the light of
the body."—Picasso

1: Sleeping Nude

Almost a Frankenstein, that tall and gaunt—
shoulders, neck and head make a right angle
of his body and parallel the ceiling;
he stands rigid above the girl sleeping
on her back, curving thighs and wide hips
up to him. The man looks angry,
as if, she, a wild animal, wandered
from the deep woods to his mattress on the floor.
But this is Paris: Nineteen four.
The door of dark and light divides
Picasso from his mistress. So ill at ease,
so located is he in this mass of dark,
so locked into his inability to know
or to possess this rectangle of pure light
she lies in, barely floating,
one might think he contemplates
killing her. Or to kill himself. One wonders
if he is thinking of her at all.

2: Meditation   A thin blue shadow spills from the cup and saucer.
And also bathed in blue, Picasso, *Le Penseur*,
shifts away from the table, has been watching
for hours, the woman sleep. Her arms
cradle her golden face. She's remote as a star,
and he is her only planet. His focus blurs.
Relaxing into light, he relaxes into her.

3:

The act, to watch you sleep, entering
your light, your light like water—
how pure the feeling is! The feeling
is like swimming. A shaky intimacy,
an act of tenderness between us,
a sort of negotiation between
the body moving, and the water.

In the ocean the nightmare fish—
held whole by pressure,
rising to thinner waters
they'd explode, anchored so deeply
sunlight never reaches them—
contain their own light:
a fluid electricity, a prey-attracting light,
flashing on in courtship or when danger
is near. Deepest in sleep, is this
the creature we look upon with horror
when we are most open, the most exposed?
Still, you sleep, accepting what the light
reveals about you, knowing I am watching.
You turn, you shift your weight,
you surface momentarily and the breath goes
out of me. Always be this open to me
when you are the most closed.

The Reader

She is lying between a page and a mountain
Turning her head, it is morning
She watches light move the mountain's shadow
A little closer to her page

The book she is reading is about a mountain
Whose landscape is turning in her eyes
It is as though a map of gestures
Is all she can remember of her past

Like the man standing up in the rowboat
reaching for her as she turned away
She remembers the sky turning into the lake
As the water went over her head

She is turning on her bed like the seasons
Whose elements are simply shaped
The mountain turns in the hand of the woman
As her other hand reaches for a page to turn

The woman's isolation is like the mountain's
They become strangers the instant she turns the page
And she watches herself turn into the gestures
She begins to recognize as her own

**This World
without Miracles**

1:

Waking in the dark the dark takes on
a kind of radiance and gives the trees
an elegant human shape. I hear
cars approach from miles away and
celebrate the personality of engines!
I imagine I hear our neighbors
breathe across our acres. The bird-hearted
pulse of the raspberry bush in bloom.
And the armor of one mosquito squeezing
through one wire square of bedroom screen.

2:          The day before you left, weeding the garden,
you looked like Adam surveying the world
his first day out of Eden. I want to be
that thin familiar rib you can't
yank out. I want it not to be that easy
to rid yourself of what is
most to be desired, complex, misunderstood.
                        Who can say
desire is not practical? The body fits,
we wear it right out of the store.
Or collide with it in the street.
Or in the night, as if by accident.

3:　　　　　　　A friend writes: "It occurs to me
I may be alone for the rest of my life.
This does not terrify me as it used to.
After the divorce, I thought my privacy
a kind of punishment, having left her.
Now I can appreciate my empty time
as a great luxury, and fill it just by
looking at things. In a room alone
my paintings seem to contemplate *me*,
seem to have more of a right to be
in the room than I do." Not objects only.
The thin chill of air in early evening.
The angle of sunlight narrowing
on the floor. "Never before to discover
I can enjoy myself so much alone
is as much a shock to me as falling in love."

"Would I bore myself, or worse, would I
knock on the door of my own house
to discover, simply, no one was home?
Or the person living there I didn't like?
Always with others inappropriately
present, always that double vision—
all the time I spent seeing through their eyes!
Their presence softened the edge
of my perception. Now I feel I am learning
how to grow into the space I was always meant
to occupy, into a self I can know."
Navigating inch by inch
what the knowable landscape provides,
I am like the astronaut spinning
deeper into space, deeper into his mind,
hurtling toward darkness to celebrate
the light his world contains.

4:          I said/ imagine yourself/ in a snapshot/
in a landscape/ you think describes/
you as you/ really are/

"The mountain peaks dissolve in clouds.
Above timberline everything is grey.
Is like the world below, is like a map.
I didn't come here for the view.

I remember colors of plateaus and hills
so recently imagined, then climbed.
My legs ache. My hands are cold.
I am thirsty for the river I waded in below.

I could drink the whole river.
I could hold a mountain in my hand.
This beauty welcomes nothing
but the edelweiss."

burns my eyes/ as if my eyes could hold/
that image of you/ the way/
stones in shade/ keep in the cold/

5:          A poet has just committed suicide.
           There are reasons, I tell my students'
           anxious faces, you may not know.
           The slow poisons working as the car idles
           start long before we turn the engine on.
                        I say I think
           despair sets the mechanism going.
           Skin is palimpsest: the child's face
           sunk indelibly into the face of the adult.

           There are no questions. One cough.
           I have disturbed the order of our class.
           I sit at the head of the table rocking
           on the hind legs of my chair,
           like a woman teetering on the ledge
           of the city's tallest public building.
                        I am afraid
           I have said too much. One hand is raised.
           A voice. A first tentative gesture.
           Their rescue nets flutter open. Make room.

6:      I feel like the man in the desert,
        approaching, always in his mind, an oasis,

        not yet knowing himself a survivor.
        One by one he carries on his back,

        (as if a man could lift a weight like that)
        all he remembers of the shapes of the world:

        a dish, an antelope, a pillar, a stair,
        the snowflake's architecture, or a pear's,

        and holding each, he feels in their contours,
        the beginnings of tenderness, and fear.

        I was raised to practice such economy
        of feeling! The way my street at night

        drew in its houses and trees like a breath.
        I wanted to be the air between the mountains

        of my parents' sleeping forms!
        I wanted to be the air you could breathe.

        I live here, where I live.
        I live in my body, which is not a man's,

        but fear, as a man does, his isolation,
        the journey in the dark where his desert is.

        I know that colors occupy the darkness;
        the inconsistent clots of red, spasms

        of violet as the forest changes seasons
        on the hill below; and I know

        my blood cannot reverse its current
        or expect the sky to drop its miracle

        of water or of manna right into my mouth.
54   I cannot carry every memory.

So like the snail I am learning patience,
my household on my back.

Only my body can move with grace
in its single room, in its fixed space,

that moves as I move, east or west,
its small space with room to spare.

Living with my hunger, I can name the fear.
Four walls are four walls anywhere.

FOUR

Sounding the Lake

"This is a remarkable
depth for so small an
area, but not an inch
of it can be spared in
the imagination."
—Thoreau

The one cloud
in a blue sky
is also the one cloud

in the lake, the feeling
of something
to be distrusted

that cloud
constantly
reinventing itself.

In long light
minnows move like stars
in shallow water.

Who can calculate
the light years
from fish to fish.

You're living
your whole life
with someone

who is more
important to you
than skin.

I watch the white
boats shift
lakeside to lakeside.

But the cloud
in the lake
is more beautiful,

its shimmer,
in which I constantly
mistake myself

and fall in. This is
how it is
with you and me.

I would rather be the lake
filling the silent
yawn of the earth

where trout
move
through clear water.

I would rather be
the trout, or
the dream of the trout,

the spasm of cloud
in the trout's brain,
oh anything but this

feeling, which is
what breaks me, friend,
when you enter.

Iowa Spring Viewed from a Plane

I will not forget how black the earth is!
The grain elevator's sharp momentary 'O'
shifts, leans away and falls
across these squared-off fields.
Occasional roads cut through.
Dot of cow, of car,
no wayward fences here, all order here,
one white farmhouse and a barn and silo
where I can almost smell the corn
going sour, as if the earth were saying
(simply) to me, "Open like these fields."
There is a table, maybe, in that kitchen
where two persons sit who are in love,
perhaps touching, perhaps not, that tension
of distance more exciting than touch;
between them a bowl with one yellow apple,
over which, the wind from the plane I'm in
makes a thin white curtain toss its shadow.

The Anniversary   Always the skull-white kitchen walls
and waxed begonia, the sill's exotic
spill of bric-a-brac traps all the daylight,
and the landscape is natural as gravity—
fields of hefty pigs I mistook for cows
our first drive out, root me,
make the real world real.
A pail rusts in the yard.
Birds are preening in the oak.

Miles from the Atlantic and yet
if I put my ear to your ear
I think I could hear the ocean.
This morning the sun flares up
clear through my eyelids,
a blizzard of light. And desire
is a thirst, a fine jewelry
clinking at the back of the neck.

The fields are misting over.
The hills assume their contours,
fringed by poplars.
Whatever provokes October to singe
the fields, lifts to the mountains
in acres of flames. In the distance
the papery farmhouse roof
goes white with heat.

Where the road slopes into town
a single birch advances into winter.
The last leaves snag the branches
like many tiny kites.
Yesterday, I saw, squashed in the road,
as if it were melting into the road,
a sparrow, the thickness
and the color of clotted leaves.
Cushioned in the nest of its own body,
only the head, that egg of a skull,
was perfect and whole in my hand.

62

Fist to your face, face to the wall,
wedged in your opaque box of sleep,
you are the absence I wake up to.
I walk into the kitchen knowing
the kitchen will be there.
I trust the chair I am sitting in
not to break. In my hand
the coffee steams, yet I feel
that rag of a bird still there,
that thinned-out tree,
each branch's arch and ache.

The Eclipse,
the Still Life
and the Painter

He wanted to describe the changes in the sky—
the landscape darkening and the shapes

on his table, roses and a bowl of fruit
becoming only fragrance.

He wanted to describe how light
became a conspiracy against his eyes

and was not a question of what he chose to see,
a cloud passing over or a mote on his eye.

The sky kept changing and displayed its stars.
The animals in the woods were confused into sleep.

He assembled the objects and mixed his colors
by candlelight in the afternoon.

The Sniper as Axis Mundi

Up up the shaky ladder to the top
the gilt dome balloons above
his ropes and buckets of whitewash
as he ducks behind the peeling columns
and begins. Every sound is a small sound.
The slap of the brush on wood
is carried off. Everything that moves
is dangerous. The river must be stopped.
Stoops and windows suddenly are sharp.
That windshield, there, glares back.
Braced and aiming now. When I squint
I see him squint. He follows the whitish
blur of my wool hat, bobbing.

Mud Season:
Vermont

Under us the white roads dissolve.
The car dives deeper into fog.
Avoiding me, your eyes are headlights.
They stab the growing dark. I am afraid
to touch you. We pass a barn collapsed.
A fat moon floods the yard. Nothing
can shatter this composure you
wear like a frosted windshield. Tense
since we argued. Around us slushy fields
split open, sea-beds, one deer stunned.
When you reach suddenly for me
somewhere inside me an iceberg cracks,
a deeper anger hardens.
Spring is here, breaking up within.

Landscape with Trees

for John and Susan
Koethe

The 'ideal reader' never gets distracted by meanings.
For example, the 'sky' is always blue or grey.
A few leafless trees interrupt the field.
No one tries to force the idea of death into autumn.

I am talking about the literal surface of, say,
the sky. Its notion of calm, its idea of itself
when approached with the thought of a 'meteor.'

We can wish to be near the ocean
and an 'ocean' appears before our very eyes!
though our vision of it is always full of errors.

What 'size,' for instance, is the bird nesting?
And, in what 'kind' of tree?
The tree I imagine you can only approximate.

I am probably sitting in a house with a view.
The literalness of 'the window' can only be guessed at
when the bird of this poem chooses to fly through.

**The Necklace
of Anger**

If I could wear my anger around my neck,
that ugly jewelry clinking, clinking,
it'd be strung with teeth: strong chewers
of mukluks, teeth that twist off
bottletops, shark and tiger teeth, sets
of chattering false teeth, the funny ones
you wind up to mow the lawn.

When I'd walk,
I'd walk with a terrible loudness.
I'd ask the dentist to fill each tooth
with a silver microphone. My sensitive
necklace would pick up all the sounds
in my head. You'd hear great cyclones
of breath and the motes that slide
across my eyes like continents.

And still I think I might scare myself
with the noise I make. Something quieter,
a blizzard inside a glass paperweight,
offends no one. Facing you when I am angriest,
I wouldn't need to be articulate or move
an inch. There I'd sit, wearing my necklace
around my throat, a string
of covered wagons when you attack.

Survival Tactics

"The most primitive
animals need not fall
in love." *A Child is
Born*: Nilsson

"Dangerous," he says, "I am dangerous
to women. I must be kept
away from them." He does not say,
"You terrify, you astonish me."
Houdini, heart-breaker,
"a chain of broken hearts
five miles long," I sing
over Bloody Marys in a bar.
Winged, we move out in the wind
whipping in from Boston Harbor.

His bedroom's done up as a cave.
Collapsing into goosedown,
his one arm pulls me toward him,
the other pushes me away.
The ceiling is so low
I can feel the peeled paint craters,
some touchable moon!

Oh, he is swimming upstream to me.
"No," he says, "we're those deep-sea fish
who shy away from light
growing stranger, less intimate
the deeper in we go."

"But we are a colonial order
like coral reefs," I say.
"No," he says. "Corals extrude
their sex cells into water
without ceremony, without ceremony."

"And jellyfish," I say.
He: "At times, amphibians produce ova
when the males are far away."
"Their courtship is elaborate," I say.

He says, "Loving you is dangerous."
We disconnect. He says,
"And terrible. I read someplace
enough ova to provide

the present world population
could fill a silk top hat.
And the sperm to fertilize it
could fill a thimble."

"A thimbleful in me," I say.

Landing Off Season

Jetties extend sturdy gangplanks
to the rows of evacuated bungalows
the rigid gulls coast over. In the wake
of another winter tracing your yard,
one skimpy hedge.
The porch light makes all the blues
green, the greens blue, your skin
yellowish. Your fingers have a weave
where you press the kitchen screen.
All afternoon the propped sweet
potato sprawled from the cloudy glass
you toyed with, and in the dark
I could see how privacy was torture,
my visit, a kind disruption of trees
in tall grass. Now we joke, dismantling
a lobster. The butter grits.
I can locate isolation on any map.
Everywhere I step is a staircase
to sabotage. You will know. When I survive,
this leaf, here, bends toward light.

FIVE

Eye Level

For Mary W. Sheldon

If exposed to total
darkness for 72 hours,
the retina degenerates,
causing partial loss
of vision.

1: North

Wisteria worked its patient violence on the house.
Working at civility, we moved
from room to room like diplomats,
dividing china, dismantling the easy chair.
Out from the linen closet, the tent collapsed
to a small bag of telescoping poles; the compass;
the Coleman stove's blue bracelet of flame.
Your Swiss Army knife tamed any emergency—
miniature corkscrew, screwdriver, fish scaler, file—
all blades snapped into that miracle of steel.
I slipped it in my pocket, the red handle
shining like a deep wound in my palm. Only this
I kept to cut my narrow path away from you.

2: Haiti:
Skin Diving

My legs break
the thick glass floor
of water.

My foot magnifies
blue as the foot
of a corpse.

One unshuttable eye
spans my face
and sees easily

what two eyes
can hardly see.
I breathe

and go under.
Sea urchins fan
black sprays of quills.

Sea fans sway
at right angles
to the current.

My snorkel's ball
spins in its atmosphere
of breath

like tiny Mars
above my head.
The sixth sense

must be gravity!
I measure distance
now by fin-kicks,

by the sun's angle.
Finned, the swimmer
wades backwards

to the sea,
waist-deep, to plunge
and turn almost

weightless inside
the moving
body once again.

All the lyre-tailed,
stippled, rainbow-
flecked bodies

flash—shaped by water.
A school of fish
spills from the coral

and circles me.
I stiffen
without moving.

My fingertip's
slightest tremor
could shatter that order,

blurring
as my breath
clouds the mask.

3: Port-au-Prince   In the thatched *choucoune*,
                     I learned Creole proverbs
                     from the maid. *The fish*
                     trusts the water and in the water
                     it is cooked.

                     Was that thunder in the harbor?
                     Smoke funneled from the Iron Market.
                     The gardener shinnied up a palm tree
                     like a sailor up a mast,
                     my binoculars bouncing against his back.
                     The maid translated his shouts
                     half in Creole, half in French,
                     and still I could not connect.
                     I telephoned the Embassy—
                     heard, fractured by static,
                     ". . . an old military plane
                     crashed in the street,
                     skidding into a *tap-tap*
                     jammed with passengers."

                     When the hawk strikes
                     if he doesn't take feathers
                     he takes straw.

                     All varieties of blood
                     bloom at eye level. *Flamboyant.*
                     Belle Mexicaine. Acres of poinsettia
                     flame up the cliffs
                     along the Kenscoff Road.

                     The last hurricane
                     cut the banana plantation down.
                     The way an image
                     inverts inside the eye,
                     I saw bunches of bananas jutting
                     like chandeliers out of the ground.
                     The palace leveled by jungle,
                     accessible only by air.
                     This violence civilized
78   by machete, jeep and climate.

4: Blackout

Only the knife knows
what is in the heart
of the yam.

A blazing eye
will not set the house
on fire.

All electric power blew;
I swung the shutters
open and leaned

over the fretwork
of the balcony,
as the city

sank—tier
by brilliant tier—
into the harbor.

Stumbling toward
the door, my fingers
on the braille plaster

of the walls, until
my bare feet
felt the landing,

the wooden boxes
of the steps.
In my hand,

my butane lighter
slid a small circle
down the stairs,

and the stairs
became all motion,
surfaces angled

off to surfaces
I couldn't see;
and I, suddenly

brave among shadows,
yelled out
to scare the maid,

"Esprit! Esprit!"
thinking it meant
'ghost' . . .

*Save yourself
from drowning.
The day a leaf
falls in the water
may not be
the day it sinks.*

5: North: The Fish

The blind and
depigmented fish,
Amblyopsis spelaea,
inhabits streams in
the dark zones of
caves in southern
Indiana.

In the laboratory, the scientist
explains what I am about to see.
How, in Huddelson's cornfield,
the farmer discovered the cave
when his pig fell in the hole.
Lowered by rope into a twilit chamber,
the scientist landed on a dirt mound
studded with lost things: a hoe, twisted
vertebrae, and keys, shreds of tinfoil—
whatever shiny caught the pack rats' eyes.

The scientist shuts off the lights
and guides me one step up, unbolting
a room of cold and dark so dense
its clarity shocks instantly—
as in the nightmare dive, the dreamer
wakes mid-air over water.
In the frozen halo of my iris,
the dark target widens.

Total darkness isn't black,
but is a deep and pit-like grey
that draws the eye into its depths.
The scientist passes me the flashlight
like a cigarette. Each fish
looks like a finger's length of quartz.
The colorless scales have the sheen
of silk, and silver mesh around the gills.
The fins, thin undulant fans, quiver.
If you should cut one open,
its blood would run clear as water.
Light shines straight through its head.
I focus on where the eyes should be.
The skin stretches unbroken over the skull,
flat and smooth as a thumbnail.
The sockets are shadows trapped in ice.

81

I dip my hand into the water
to touch the glacial head.
The fish darts away!
It stuns like current as I jerk back,
my hand rigid at my side.
My eye burns beyond its chemicals.

6:          Across the garden
two birds call
into my sleep.

What was it
I was dreaming?
—a mermaid turning

in your net
you wished to make
human by an act

of love? Landlocked,
I was only
divided by desire.

In sleep,
when each has lost
the enterprise of

self, and the heart
no longer steers
within the body's

limits, then
sun, moon and skull
are equal in the mind.

On a sea bed, or bed
of linen, the same
skeletal thrash

in darkness:
to choke on water
as on air.

Desire's
just the interval
in birdsong.

The two call
across the distance
of the bed.

The voices call
despite weather
or temperament.

I let you go.
But see how my desire
drew you in.

7: *Trompe-l'oeil*   Tonight, the grid
of trolley wires
that canopies the street

sags under
the sky's dark weight.
I glanced out

the window the moment
the trolley passed—
spattering an enormous

blue-white spark
that filled my bedroom
like pistolshot—

branding trees,
the house opposite,
where still cars

bloomed in points
of light. Surveying
the injury, I focussed

on the dark.
Trees uprooted, cars
parked in air.

Everywhere I looked
their outlines
shocked the dark

and floated exactly
as they were:
double-exposed on

the ceiling, the wall,
then burning against
the back of my hand.

Was I looking
at tomorrow, daylight
out of any time,

or history
repeating itself
in waves?

In seconds,
the image began
to fade.

What the eye cannot
hold, it holds
and sharpens

in memory, when
a detail overlooked
ignites

on the white periphery.
The glitter of
things outside

short-circuiting
beyond sight.
The spark deepening

in the brain
as the dark grows
more intense,

when, for an instant,
light's all
that's permanent.